How to create a Graph on Google Sheets

A beginner's guide

by Jobs Timer

Table of Contents

VI. Choosing the Chart Type
A. Exploring various chart types (line, bar, pie, etc.)
B. Selecting the most appropriate chart type for the data

VII. Customizing the Graph
A. Adjusting chart title and axis titles
B. Changing colors and styles
C. Adding data labels and annotations

VIII. Interpreting the Graph
A. Understanding the visual representation of data
B. Analyzing trends and patterns

IX. Updating Data in the Graph
A. Editing the data in the spreadsheet
B. Seeing automatic updates in the graph

X. Sharing the Graph
A. Sharing options in Google Sheets
B. Collaborating with others

I. Introduction

A. Explanation of Google Sheets

Google Sheets is a web-based spreadsheet application developed by Google.

It allows users to create, edit, and collaborate on spreadsheets in real-time through a web browser.

Google Sheets offers a wide range of functionalities similar to traditional spreadsheet software like Microsoft Excel, including data manipulation, formula calculations, and chart creation.

B. Importance of visualizing data with graphs

Visualizing data with graphs is crucial for effectively conveying information and insights derived from data.

Graphs provide a visual representation of data patterns, trends, and relationships, making it easier for users to interpret and understand complex data sets.

Some key reasons why visualizing data with graphs is important include:

Clarity and Interpretation:

Graphs simplify complex data sets into easily understandable visual representations, allowing users to quickly grasp trends and patterns without extensive data analysis.

Comparison and Analysis:

Graphs enable users to compare different data sets or variables visually, facilitating analysis and decision-making processes.

Communication:

Visual representations of data are often more engaging and persuasive than raw numbers or text, making it easier to communicate findings and insights to stakeholders.

Identification of Trends:

Graphs help identify trends, outliers, and anomalies in data sets, which can provide valuable insights for decision-making and problem-solving.

Forecasting and Prediction:

Graphical representations of historical data can aid in forecasting future trends and making predictions based on past patterns.

Overall, visualizing data with graphs in tools like Google Sheets enhances data comprehension, facilitates analysis, and improves decision-making processes across various domains and industries.

II. Accessing Google Sheets

A. Opening Google Sheets in a web browser

To access Google Sheets in a web browser, follow these steps:

Launch your preferred web browser (e.g., Google Chrome, Mozilla Firefox, Safari).

In the address bar, type "sheets.google.com" and press Enter.

If you're not already signed in to your Google account, you'll be prompted to sign in.

Enter your email address and password associated with your Google account.

Once signed in, you'll be redirected to the Google Sheets homepage where you can create new spreadsheets or access existing ones.

B. Signing in to your Google account

If you're not already signed in to your Google account, follow these steps to sign in:

On the Google Sheets homepage or any Google Sheets document, click on the "Sign In" button located at the top right corner of the screen.

Enter your email address associated with your Google account and click "Next."

Enter your password and click "Next" to sign in.

Once signed in, you'll have access to all the features of Google Sheets, including creating, editing, and sharing spreadsheets with others.

III. Entering Data

A. Creating a new spreadsheet

To create a new spreadsheet in Google Sheets, follow these steps:

Open Google Sheets in your web browser by navigating to "sheets.google.com" and signing in to your Google account if you're not already signed in.

Once on the Google Sheets homepage, click on the "+ Blank" or "Blank" button to create a new, empty spreadsheet.

A new spreadsheet will open in a new tab or window, ready for you to start entering data.

B. Entering data into cells

To enter data into cells in Google Sheets, follow these steps:

Click on the cell where you want to enter data. The selected cell will be highlighted.

Type the data you want to enter into the selected cell. You can enter text, numbers, dates, or formulas.

Press Enter on your keyboard or click on another cell to confirm and move to the next cell. Your entered data will be saved in the selected cell.

Repeat these steps for each cell where you want to enter data. You can also use keyboard shortcuts like Tab to move to the next cell or Shift+Tab to move to the previous cell for faster data entry.

Additionally, you can copy and paste data from other sources such as text documents, spreadsheets, or websites into Google Sheets.

Simply select the data you want to copy, right-click, choose "Copy," then click on the destination cell in Google Sheets and right-click to choose "Paste" or use the keyboard shortcut Ctrl+V (Command+V on Mac) to paste the data.

IV. Selecting Data for the Graph

A. Highlighting the data range

To highlight the data range in Google Sheets for creating a graph, follow these steps:

Click and drag your mouse to select the range of cells that contain the data you want to include in the graph.

Alternatively, you can click on the first cell of the range, then hold down the Shift key and click on the last cell of the range to select all cells in between.

Ensure that the selected data range includes all the data you want to visualize in the graph.

You can adjust the selection by clicking and dragging the edges of the highlighted range or by clicking on individual cells while holding down the Ctrl key (Command key on Mac) to add or remove cells from the selection.

B. Choosing columns or rows for the graph

Once you've highlighted the data range, you can choose whether to create the graph using columns or rows as the series for the graph.

Here's how:

If your data is organized with categories or labels in rows and corresponding values in columns, you may want to create a graph using columns as series.

This is suitable for data where each column represents a different category or variable, and each row represents individual data points or observations.

If your data is organized with categories or labels in columns and corresponding values in rows, you may want to create a graph using rows as series.

This is suitable for data where each row represents a different category or variable, and each column represents individual data points or observations.

To choose columns or rows for the graph series:

After selecting the data range, click on the "Insert" menu at the top of the Google Sheets interface.

Select "Chart" from the dropdown menu. This will open the "Chart editor" sidebar.

In the "Chart editor" sidebar, under the "Data" tab, you'll see options for choosing columns or rows as series, depending on how your data is organized.

Click on the appropriate option (e.g., "Switch rows/columns") to toggle between using columns or rows as series for the graph.

Preview and customize your graph settings as needed in the "Chart editor" sidebar, then click "Insert" to insert the graph into your spreadsheet.

By following these steps, you can easily select the data range and choose columns or rows for the graph in Google Sheets, enabling you to visualize your data effectively.

V. Inserting a Graph

A. Clicking on "Insert" from the menu

To insert a graph in Google Sheets, follow these steps:

Ensure that you have selected the data range you want to visualize as a graph.

Click on the "Insert" menu located at the top of the Google Sheets interface.

B. Selecting "Chart" from the dropdown menu

Once you've clicked on the "Insert" menu, follow these steps to select "Chart" from the dropdown menu:

After clicking on the "Insert" menu, a dropdown menu will appear.

From the dropdown menu, select "Chart." This will open the "Chart editor" sidebar.

Following these steps will open the "Chart editor" sidebar, where you can customize various aspects of your chart, such as chart type, data range, titles, axes, and more.

You can then preview and customize your graph settings before inserting the chart into your spreadsheet.

VI. Choosing the Chart Type

A. Exploring various chart types (line, bar, pie, etc.)

Google Sheets offers a variety of chart types to visualize data effectively.

Here are some commonly used chart types:

Line Chart:

Displays data points connected by straight lines. It's useful for showing trends over time or continuous data.

Bar Chart:

Represents data using rectangular bars, with the length of each bar proportional to the value it represents. It's suitable for comparing values across categories.

Column Chart:

Similar to a bar chart, but the bars are vertical instead of horizontal. It's also used for comparing values across categories.

Pie Chart:

Shows data as slices of a circular pie, with each slice representing a proportion of the whole. It's effective for illustrating parts of a whole or showing percentages.

Area Chart:

Similar to a line chart, but the area below the line is filled with color. It's useful for emphasizing the magnitude of change over time.

Scatter Chart:

Displays individual data points as dots, with the position of each dot determined by its x and y values. It's used to show relationships between two variables.

Histogram:

Presents data distribution by grouping values into bins or intervals along the x-axis and showing the frequency of occurrences on the y-axis. It's helpful for analyzing data distribution and identifying patterns.

Combo Chart:

Combines two or more chart types in a single chart, allowing for the comparison of different data series.

B. Selecting the most appropriate chart type for the data

Choosing the most appropriate chart type depends on the nature of your data and the message you want to convey.

Here are some considerations to help you select the right chart type:

Data Structure:

Consider how your data is structured and what relationships you want to highlight.

For example, if you're comparing values across categories, a bar or column chart may be suitable. If you're showing trends over time, a line chart might be more appropriate.

Message Clarity:

Choose a chart type that makes it easy for your audience to understand the main message of your data.

Avoid clutter and complexity that could confuse the viewer.

Data Size:

Some chart types are better suited for large datasets, while others are more effective for smaller datasets.

Consider the size of your data and whether the chosen chart type can effectively represent it.

Audience Preference:

Take into account the preferences and familiarity of your audience with different chart types.

Choose a chart type that your audience will find easy to interpret and engage with.

By considering these factors, you can select the most appropriate chart type that effectively communicates your data and insights to your audience.

VII. Customizing the Graph

A. Adjusting chart title and axis titles

To customize the title and axis titles of your graph in Google Sheets, follow these steps:

Click on the graph to select it. You should see handles and options appear around the chart.

Click on the "Chart editor" button (it looks like a small pencil) in the upper-right corner of the chart. This will open the Chart editor sidebar.

In the "Chart editor" sidebar, navigate to the "Customize" tab.

Under the "Chart & axis titles" section, you can customize the chart title, horizontal axis title, and vertical axis title by clicking on the text boxes and entering your desired titles.

Once you've entered your desired titles, you can further customize the font, size, color, and alignment of the titles using the options available in the "Chart & axis titles" section.

B. Changing colors and styles

To change the colors and styles of your graph elements in Google Sheets, follow these steps:

Click on the graph to select it.

Click on the "Chart editor" button to open the Chart editor sidebar.

In the "Chart editor" sidebar, navigate to the "Customize" tab.

Under the "Series" section, you can customize the colors, line thickness, and other styles for each series in your graph.

You can also customize the background color, gridlines, and other visual elements of the chart by navigating to the "Chart style" section in the "Customize" tab.

C. Adding data labels and annotations

To add data labels and annotations to your graph in Google Sheets, follow these steps:

Click on the graph to select it.

Click on the "Chart editor" button to open the Chart editor sidebar.

In the "Chart editor" sidebar, navigate to the "Customize" tab.

Under the "Series" section, you can toggle the "Data labels" option to display labels for each data point in your graph.

To add annotations, navigate to the "Annotations" section in the "Customize" tab.

Click on the "+" button to add a new annotation, then enter your annotation text and customize its appearance as desired.

VIII. Interpreting the Graph

A. Understanding the visual representation of data

Interpreting a graph involves understanding the visual representation of data to extract meaningful insights.

Here are key aspects to consider:

Data Representation: Identify what the x-axis and y-axis represent.

The x-axis typically represents categories or time intervals, while the y-axis represents numerical values.

Chart Type:

Consider the type of graph used and how it represents the data. For example, a line graph shows trends over time, while a bar graph compares values across categories.

Data Points:

Each point on the graph represents a specific data value. Pay attention to the position of data points relative to the axes and other data points.

Trends and Patterns:

Look for trends, patterns, and relationships between data points. Are there noticeable increases or decreases over time? Are there any outliers or anomalies?

Title and Labels:

Read the chart title and axis labels to understand the context of the data and what the graph is illustrating.

B. Analyzing trends and patterns

Analyzing trends and patterns involves examining the data represented in the graph to draw insights and conclusions. Here's how to analyze trends and patterns effectively:

Identify Trends:

Look for overall trends in the data. Are there consistent increases, decreases, or fluctuations over time or across categories?

Spot Anomalies:

Identify any outliers or anomalies in the data. These could indicate unusual events or errors in data collection.

Compare Data Sets:

If the graph contains multiple data sets or series, compare them to each other. Look for differences, similarities, and relationships between the data sets.

Consider Context:

Take into account the context of the data and any external factors that may influence the trends and patterns observed in the graph.

Draw Conclusions:

Based on your analysis, draw conclusions about the data. What insights can be gleaned from the trends and patterns observed? Are there any implications or actionable insights?

IX. Updating Data in the Graph

A. Editing the data in the spreadsheet

To update the data in the graph in Google Sheets, you need to edit the corresponding data in the spreadsheet. Follow these steps:

Open your Google Sheets document containing the data used in the graph. Locate the cells containing the data you want to update.

Edit the values in the cells as needed. You can either type directly into the cells or use formulas to calculate new values.

Once you've made the necessary changes, the data in the spreadsheet will be updated.

B. Seeing automatic updates in the graph

Google Sheets automatically updates the graph to reflect any changes made to the underlying data in the spreadsheet.

You should see the graph update in real-time as you edit the data in the spreadsheet.

If you don't see automatic updates in the graph:

Ensure that you've saved your changes to the spreadsheet by clicking the "Save" button or using the keyboard shortcut Ctrl + S (Command + S on Mac).

Check that the data range used in the graph includes the updated data.

If you've added or removed rows or columns in the spreadsheet, you may need to adjust the data range in the graph settings.

If you've made significant changes to the data structure or the chart type, you may need to re-insert the graph to ensure it reflects the updated data correctly.

By editing the data in the spreadsheet, you can see automatic updates in the graph, allowing you to visualize changes and trends in your data effectively.

X. Sharing the Graph

A. Sharing options in Google Sheets

Google Sheets offers various options for sharing graphs with others.

Here's how to access sharing options:

Share Button: Click on the "Share" button located in the top-right corner of the Google Sheets interface.

This button typically looks like a silhouette of a person with a "+" sign.

Link Sharing:

You can generate a shareable link that allows anyone with the link to view the spreadsheet and the associated graph.

You can set permissions for the link, such as allowing viewers to only view the spreadsheet or allowing them to edit it as well.

Email Sharing:

You can enter email addresses directly to share the spreadsheet and graph with specific individuals.

You can also set permissions for each person, such as viewer, commenter, or editor.

Advanced Sharing Settings:

Google Sheets provides advanced sharing settings where you can manage permissions for specific individuals or groups. You can control who can view, comment, or edit the spreadsheet and associated graphs.

B. Collaborating with others

Google Sheets facilitates collaboration by allowing multiple users to work on the same spreadsheet simultaneously. Here's how to collaborate with others:

Share the Spreadsheet:

Use the sharing options mentioned above to share the spreadsheet containing the graph with others. You can invite collaborators via email or share a link with them.

Real-Time Collaboration:

When collaborators access the shared spreadsheet, they can make edits to the data or graph in real-time. Each collaborator's changes are automatically synced, allowing everyone to see the updates instantly.

Comments and Suggestions:

Collaborators can leave comments and suggestions on specific cells, graphs, or the entire spreadsheet. This feature facilitates communication and feedback among collaborators.

Revision History:

Google Sheets keeps track of the revision history, allowing you to see who made changes to the spreadsheet and when. You can revert to previous versions if needed.

By utilizing sharing options and collaboration features in Google Sheets, you can easily share graphs with others and work together on data analysis and visualization projects.

Printed in Great Britain
by Amazon

42915613R10030